Martin Murphy

Villain

D1381637

Bloomsbury Methuen Drama
An imprint of Bloomsbury Publishing Plc

BLOOMSBURY
LONDON • OXFORD • NEW YORK • NEW DELHI • SYDNEY

Bloomsbury Methuen Drama

An imprint of Bloomsbury Publishing Plc

Imprint previously known as Methuen Drama

50 Bedford Square
London
WC1B 3DP
UK

1385 Broadway
New York
NY 10018
USA

www.bloomsbury.com

BLOOMSBURY, METHUEN DRAMA **and the Diana logo
are trademarks of Bloomsbury Publishing Plc**

First published 2017

© Martin Murphy, 2017

British Library Cataloguing-in-Publication Data
A catalogue record for this book is available from the British Library.

ISBN: PB: 978-1-3500-3747-2
e-PDF: 978-1-3500-3746-5
ePub: 978-1-3500-3748-9

Library of Congress Cataloging in Publication Data
A catalog record for this book is available from the Library of Congress

Series: Modern Plays

Typeset by Country Setting, Kingsdown, Kent CT14 8ES
Printed and bound in Great Britain

Cover design: Olivia D'Cruz
Cover image and image design © Bruised Sky Productions

To find out more about our authors and books visit www.bloomsbury.com.
Here you will find extracts, author interviews, details of forthcoming events
and the option to sign up for our newsletters.

**Bruised Sky Productions
present**

VILLAIN

by Martin Murphy

Villain

presented by
Bruised Sky Productions

RACHEL   Maddie Rice

Director   Martin Murphy

*Sound and
Lighting Designer*   Kevin Millband

*Associate Producer
and Dramaturg*   Jules Haworth

Associate Producer   Hannah Cox

Artistic Director   James Kermack

Villain previewed at Soho Theatre, London,
on 2 August 2016, before opening at Underbelly,
Edinburgh, on 4 August 2016

Villain was revived at the King's Head Theatre,
London, in February 2017

Bruised Sky Productions

Bruised Sky Productions was founded by Artistic Director James Kermack in 2009 with Executive Director Martin Murphy appointed later that year. The company's first production, *Lads,* received a range of five- and four-star reviews at the Edinburgh Fringe Festival before a London run at the Canal Cafe.

Bruised Sky most recently presented *Worlds* at VAULT Festival in January 2017, following the success of *Villain* at the Edinburgh Fringe Festival, 2016.

Bruised Sky's other works include: *Manor* by Martin Murphy, which played at Soho Theatre before a three-week run at Tristan Bates Theatre, Covent Garden, and *Animal Bordello* written by David Scinto, writer of the Oscar-nominated classic, *Sexy Beast*.

Creative Team

Writer/Director | Martin Murphy

Martin's plays include: *Worlds* (VAULT Festival, 2017), *Manor* (Soho Theatre, 2009) and *Barren* (Old Vic Theatre, OVNV 24 Hour Plays, 2006). Martin has also written the short film *Poisoned* and numerous other short plays at venues including the Liverpool Everyman Theatre and The Old Vic.

As a performer, Martin is half of the musical comedy double act Pistol and Jack who have performed at a large number of venues including Secret Garden Party, Assembly Edinburgh, Nu:Write Festival Zagreb and Soho Theatre.

Performer | Maddie Rice

Maddie trained at Mountview Academy of Theatre Arts. Her theatre credits include: *Fleabag* (UK tour), *Henry V* (MGC/West End), *All My Sons* (Regent's Park Open Air Theatre), *News Revue* (Edinburgh, Pleasance), *zazU: A Fete Worse than Death* (Soho Theatre), A *Midsummer Night's Dream*, *The Taming of the Shrew* and *Macbeth* (Principal Theatre). Her television credits include: *I Live With Models* (Comedy Central), *Call The Midwife*, and *Who killed Laura Kitchens?* (BBC). Maddie also writes and performs with comedy groups zazU and Lead Pencil.

Lighting and Sound Designer | Kevin Millband

Kevin trained in Literature and Imaginative Writing and has since worked as a technician and sound and lighting designer in venues across London and at the Edinburgh Fringe Festival. Kevin is also Production Manager of the award-winning Crafternoon Cabaret Club.

Associate Producer and Dramaturg | Jules Haworth

Jules is Education Producer at Soho Theatre and runs the Writers' Lab and Comedy Lab programmes for emerging artists. Dramaturgy credits include: *Brute* by Izzy Tennyson (Ideas Tap Underbelly Award 2015), *Muscovado* by Matilda Ibini (Alfred Fagon Award 2015), *In Your Image* by Gemma Copping (Soho Theatre Young Writers' Award 2013), *On the Edge of Me* by Yolanda Mercy (tour) and *The Dogs of War* by Tim Foley (Old Red Lion). Jules' play *Pigeon Steps* was longlisted for the Adrian Pagan Award 2014.

Associate Producer | Hannah Cox

Hannah is Young People's Programme Manager at the National Theatre and has been working in Arts Education for twelve years. She has extensive experience programming and producing for Southbank Centre, Soho Theatre, and numerous smaller organisations, as well as running her own company, Crafternoon Cabaret Club. Hannah is a passionate advocate for political theatre and new writing.

Artistic Director | James Kermack

James has been Artistic Director of Bruised Sky since forming the company in 2009. He wrote and directed the critically acclaimed five-star play *Lads* before directing Martin Murphy's play, *Manor*. James also directed over forty theatre productions as a freelance director before moving into film and television.

His debut feature film, *Hi-Lo Joe*, completed in 2015, was chosen to be a part of Film London Breakthrough playing at the BFI Southbank in 2016 and had its world premiere at the prestigious 27th Dinard British Film Festival, where James was also a jury member. His second feature, the multi-million-pound action thriller *Knuckledust*, shoots across three countries in 2017. In September 2016, James was announced as Head of Creative Development at Featuristic films.

Special thanks to

Becci Gemmell, Sue Smith, Alan Stratford, Soho Theatre,
Byroc Play Productions Ltd, Hannah Cox, Rosie Smith,
Julia Murray, Chantelle Dusette, Georgia Sykes, Karen Fisher,
Theatre Royal Stratford East, the King's Head Theatre,
James Kermack and all the people that gave individually or
via our Indiegogo campaign and made this production possible.

Villain

Characters

Rachel

Author's Note

Although locations are occasionally described in the text, in no way is it my intention for the set to accurately recreate these. The play favours a non-naturalistic staging although this is obviously at the discretion of individual directors.

Punctuation and spelling are used to indicate delivery, not to conform to the rules of grammar.

Scene One

*House lights go down and we hear a chant of 'Scum. Scum. Scum',
which gets louder as music fades.*

We see **Rachel**, *a smartly dressed woman sitting alone.*

Rachel Always start with the end. Always, start with the
end. So here it is and here I am. On the Tube they spotted me.
Bank, interchange with DLR. Fucking hate South London.
Someone had a copy of the *Standard*, I wasn't front page.
Unusual, well at the moment it's unusual but a plane had
crashed and we're speculating as to whether it's been done
on purpose. Well the papers are. Someone from here, jihadis.
On Tube. Two folks had a row, reckoned there was more
space, think he could have moved down. Blokes, lock horns,
goes nowhere but makes a fella sat down nervous, he's a
nervous type, looks at the situation then his paper then to me.
Then to his paper then back to me and he's seen. Yeah he's
seen what he's thought he's seen, page seven there it is and
there I am. Monster. Off train. Escalator. Exits. Folk giving out
the *Standard*. Me walking. Fast. Suits. Blokes in suits walking in
front of me. Blocking my way. Walking two-by-two but wide.
Walking wide I can't overtake them. I go in the road. Walk
middle of the streets. My streets. Fuck 'em. Bastards. Alleyway
and I can slow down. Catch my breath. I'm OK. I move inside.
Head office, high ceilings, low morals. Security guard greets
me. Friendly. I sit down, look to him 'I'm here to meet . . .'
'I know,' he says. I stand back up then sit, perch. Breathe.

The man at the desk says something. I've been sat there for a
while. He says something. 'You can go up,' he says, 'They're
ready for you.' I sit back in my chair. The chair. Recline. Then
I'm up I'm walking. Enter the room. I sit here. I'm sat here.

Then we're before.

Scene Two

Rachel   Music, loud night club, dancing. I'm twenty-two.

Dancing, she indicates a drink in her hand as she talks to a friend we cannot see.

No I've still got this one. Cheers. What? Yeah yeah, probably. Listen, have you got anywhere lined up to move into after your place runs out? When you got to have moved by? Have ya? Your parents sorting that or? Right right. No, I know I've left it a bit late maybe but gonna start looking tomorrow. I really don't wanna move home in between you know? You know, now I'm in London I might as well . . . Seems as this is where I wanna be would rather just . . . Exactly. I'd need a job though, for rent and what have ya. Think my dad would help a deposit but I need something. Who has? Has she? I'll speak to . . .

Music stops mid-sentence as she turns back to us and out of the club she has been inhabiting.

My friend Lorell told me to talk to Sarah, our friend who'd lived with us second year, graduated year before us and had jobs going in a call centre doing sales. Boring as fuck apparently but all right money and always looking for people. Always to the point where by I went to speak to her that night and she told me to come in the next day. Not like come in for an interview as in come in and start working. They didn't bother with interviews or even CVs or any kind of process at all as far as I could see. They just needed bodies. I'd never really thought what I'd do after uni, thought something would just, happen. I went in the next day, reckoned I'd be in half an hour or an hour whatever for a chat or some training at most but they had me go straight in. I was pretty hungover and nervous, but I did all right I thought, and Sarah said I'd done really well. I went for drinks with her after work and she paid at an all right place, not like where billionaires go but it wasn't student pub or a bar full of old men. it was . . . Well there were successful working people there and no one was pouring their own vodka into a Coke under the table. People just looked, well happyish. Comfortable.

It turned out there was kind of a spare room going at Sarah's. They had a four-bed place which three of them lived in and they kind of sub-let the other room out just on weekends to American tourists happy to pay over the odds for a real experience of living in London for a few days. Thing was one of these Yankee tourist girls had brought a lad back at the weekend who had . . . Well he'd thrown up while going down on her and it had caused a bit of a situation in the house. A fracas. So the three girls had decided maybe they should just have one full-time person to minimise risk of crazy weekend Americans. So within basically two days of handing in my last bit of coursework at uni I had a job and a place to live with nice professional young women. Couldn't really complain. Also they changed the mattress after, well, the girl before me's incident.

Scene Three

Rachel   I'm awake, finally. Unless I think I'm awake. I can't move. I can't move I can't move. Fuck. No I'm not awake am I. Am I? No. Try again. Move my arm, move my arm and I can't I'm trapped. I'm trapped. I keep waking up like this I think it's when you're in one dream and you're not liking it so you try to wake yourself up, I have dreams where in the dream I'm pulling my eyelids apart trying to make myself be awake, to snap out of it. I thought I'd done this, got my eyes open so I could see the room. Then there was this rat, in the ceiling, a rat coming through the paint but not like it actually would if it was scratching through, more like if a rat had been dipped in paint and was coming through towards you. So I knew once I saw it was coming towards my face like that I hated it but I knew it wasn't real. That horrible as it was, scary as it was, this was just a dream and that when I woke up the real life I had. The real world outside my head was so much fucking worse.

I get out the house, long coat and a hat, it's the middle of the night and no paps waiting outside the house at the moment. I know newspapers' job is to let let people know the things going on in the world and that means some Godawful horrible things as well as the nice ones obviously but it's hard to understand how a footballer shagging behind his family's back while he's winning some Dad of the Year award and an actor getting a co-star he's had an affair with sacked because his wife doesn't want him working with her any more get injunctioned but they can say where I work and publish photos of me coming out of my home.

I'm walking along Parkway in Camden. I'm walking up towards Regent's Park and there's the place on the left, it's a nice restaurant now, well I've heard it's nice I've never been but I'm told, the food is very nice. The building was the off-licence, it's closed. It's been closed for years now and it makes me wonder how can it be empty? There must be so many shops want that site and it's derelict. I could go there some time, bolted up, chained off. If I can get myself in there. No one would be looking for me. I could be safe.

Scene Four

Rachel   Green. Lanes. Long road. Long fucking road. Long fucking road and I'm walking it. Walking it why? Cos that's how we get to cases or we use public transport, which we pay for ourselves pretty much. I feel? I feel all right actually. Actually considering. I feel all right. I speak to this dad, seems fine, seems fine have to barrel through, as I leave as I close the door then hear 'Why you say that in front of the lady?' Silence. The door's closed. I'm the other side, there's no more sound. Next case. I'm on my way. On to the next one. Always late for the next one. Cutting each one short, leaving early and still late for where you're supposed to be. Where you *need* to be. I'm there. Late.

There was a young girl had a son and her mum had just died, the baby's nan, and so the girl was really down, you would be. And neighbours were saying she was getting wasted, like proper drunk and the baby was just crying and crying. She admitted she'd been drinking and she felt so bad about it that she'd done that it made her want to get fucked up more. But that was just a bad time, you know, she came through that. She was sad her mum had died and that makes sense. We had to drug test her and her . . . the dad not sure if they were together, he didn't live there but he was around a fair bit. All right bloke, so chilled, like so chilled. Had these long dreads and I was supposed to get hair samples off both of them cos neighbours said they were smackheads which was bollocks but you have to follow up. Hair test on this fella would be ridiculous as he's not cut his hair for I don't know like twenty years and yeah there's marijuana traces gonna show up. Across twenty years I don't think there'd be many of us could say that wouldn't be the case. But she was all right the girl, she got it together and I could see each week as I spoke to her that things were getting better for her and her little boy he'd smile, and she'd smile, at him, you couldn't help but smile back at that little boy and she missed her mum, like you would, like you miss people but she got it together. To the point I didn't need to see her any more. That's the thing, you only have long lasting visits with people you can't really help. That's hard.

Scene Five

Rachel I'm starting to hate people I work with. Not the cases. Not the people I go and see. Colleagues. My face grimaces when I see Sally. And she's all right never done anything wrong. Never been anything but kind to me. Pleasant. And I've started hating her. Thinking I hate her. And it's not just her, Sally, it's everyone, everyone who looks like they're . . . coping. Just doing same thing I do pretend to cope but I hate 'em for it. Not letting it show. Then those that are cracking, showing signs of it. I hate them too. They're weak. There's a man on this train. Well there's lots, it's packed, but one catches my eye. He's pressed his head in a corner. Between the door and the side bit which has button on to open door, he's created his own space. I'm thinking, you bastard. I want that. That space. Just anything. Any tiny amount of area which is me. Just me. I'm glaring at him. He can't see, eyes fixed on his corner. I'm glaring at him. I stop. I've dropped something, a book? Oh that fucking . . . My diary.

They're making me keep a diary. Well, a journal. A work journal, not one of them teenage girl books where you write there's a boy you hate then a few pages later he's taking you to the pictures then fingerin' ya. You have to keep it and you have to keep it up to date, they check it. I hadn't been, you see. Well it's not like I haven't got enough on my plate, so they called me in. 'How's you getting on?' they say. 'I'm fine' I says. 'Good' they reply. Ask to see the journal. I make out like I'd misunderstood that I've written a personal one, they smile. 'Well there must be a page or so which isn't. Too personal. We just need a glance.' I open the first page, the only one with any writing on. First page, top of the page 'I must focus more on . . . ' Then it's blank. The only thing I've written, I've written about concentration and it trails off. They don't smile. I have to change. I'm at King's Cross and it is packed.

Delays on the Piccadilly line due to lack of available trains. What the fuck does that mean? They can't go on bloody holiday can they? The trains. 'No coming in from the side.' My dad's a rugby fan and he'd always say that, I remember hearing him saying if he was watching a game and thinking what's he going on about? Now I get the Tube during rush hour and I know what pisses him off. It's probably a different thing in rugby but when a train comes in, you're in line with the door and someone sneaks round the side of you then by the time people have got off the train sneaky fuckers are in front of ya. Today I'm not having it though. I keep my shoulders strong and wide. Woman pushing in on edge of me but I stand my ground. She makes a sound like 'Wha', like I've pushed her, but it's her momentum coming back on her.

I'm on the train, it's rammed. Someone on here has a bike. A fold-up one but still a . . . A means of transport. I was going round on one for a bit. Few days really. The others were saying it's quickest way. 'Get yourself a bike, Rachel, it's only way you'll get around on time.' I was doing them hire bikes you get, no I'm not gonna call it that twat ex-mayor's name cos he didn't invent 'em and they're not his bikes. Riding along and just stacked it. Totally went flying. not sure if I hit something or . . . A girl asked me 'Are you OK? Can I call someone?' 'I'm fine' I says, but I'm crying. Fully-grown adult crying and pushing my bike along. I stopped riding after that. My stop. Oh and look who's in the door. Twenty people trying to get off and guess who's got her fold-up bike blocking the doors.

Scene Six

Rachel   I love talking to people. Chatting to loads of different people. I just find it fascinating. Accents, thoughts, personalities. Think it's why I was good on the phone, selling. Most of my mates there would call in sick if they had a hangover or come in hungover and just look up videos of puppies on YouTube. One girl cried, actually cried at a video of two kittens climbing out of this big sock. Crying in the office because you've seen a pet come out of a piece of footwear doesn't really help you be taken seriously.

I'd be on time. I'm always on time. My mum taught me, it's arrogant to think your time is worth more than other people's. And I dressed properly, not like power suits but I just dressed work-appropriate. Some lads would come in and they'd look, not being bad but they'd look like they had slept in what they had come in wearing.

I liked making sales, hitting targets. Mates there said I was weird for liking it and some staff I didn't know didn't like fact I was doing so well, it made bosses look into whether everyone could be working harder. I mean the job when you describe it is boring. Basically our company bought data from phone shops of people who had just got a new mobile but no insurance. We'd phone and imply, not say but allude to being from whatever network they were with and try to get them to take out a very reasonably priced insurance deal.

People don't get a cover deal in the shop, you know, you get pushed into spending more on a phone than you intend to spend on food each month so 'No.' Then you've had the phone a week and you try to take some snaps in the pub and you drop the phone and it's all right it's not broke or anything but you realise if it had you'd be lugging around a shattered phone which you can only answer by putting headphones in each time someone calls for two years so then when the nice girl who I *think* said she was from Orange calls and offers an insurance deal you take it, don't you. All I had to do was be friendly on the calls with the girls and with the boys a bit sexy, nothing pervy just lower your voice a little in tone. It's odd that, not sure why it works, essentially makes you sound more like a man but the boys it seems to just . . . Well I had the top sales record in the company.

Scene Seven

Rachel   I went back there. That off-licence. With a crowbar. Down Parkway I'm walking. I'm walking, I'm walking, I'm walking. I'm smashing open the door, I'm in. I'm inside. Words, the words smashing around my ears louder than the crowbar on the lock. Never Google yourself, sounds like one of them things you just hear them big celebrities say don't you on the chat shows? They're right, they're right and I was wrong to do that, today. I'm not on Twitter, I've got a Facebook but I made my name one nobody could find unless you knew me. Don't want cases finding you, looking up stuff about you whatever.

Twitter, like the wall of a public toilet that anyone can read and anyone can write on, anyone. Saying I should be murdered, saying I should be raped, saying where I lived, saying they would kill me, would rape me. There's no point even thinking about the logic of this, the people who write those things.

I wanna go home, no not where I live, not the place that's been shared, where I'll be hounded I wanna go home home. My Mum and Dad's, I want my mum to be annoyed with me for putting socks in the pants drawer. But the meeting's tomorrow and I can't get there and back. And they'd worry, they've heard some stuff in the papers but they don't go online and I've not told them much and they shouldn't worry. I don't want that worry, what I'm feeling, going through. I don't want them having that.

So tonight I'll be here, tonight I'll sleep with a crowbar in an abandoned off-licence and tomorrow, tomorrow won't be much better than this but the day after may be slightly, then a month after who knows and in a year, maybe in a year, maybe in a year I can have something, something close to what can be called a life back and I will be able to go to my mum and I'll look, I'll look at that picture of me on the wall with the badge and see a lady this country felt should be very proud. And I won't be alone and I won't be hated and people won't feel the need to write the very worst, the very worst about me because I'll be no one, I'll be nobody again. In a year, if only in a year I could be nobody again. And I'll walk down the streets and I'll be totally ignored. But tonight, that's not tonight, so tonight I'll keep this crowbar close.

Scene Eight

Rachel You like a guy? You go up and kiss him. Or just stand near. No disrespect to whatever per cent of population have penises but they're not bright are they? A situation where there's drinks, ideally but . . . I mean I'm not suggesting that if you go stand next to a fella at the bus stop you'll end up snogging but if you're wearing a short skirt . . . ? Blokes will just start talking to you. Can you imagine being that thick? Like I might walk past a cake shop and see a Belgian bun or something and think I'd quite like that but I don't just stare at it, or try to touch it. And again no disrespect but half the population are basically morons and you can use that. I know some girls who get angry about it or try to change it or think they can. You're not gonna make men any brighter are you? No brighter than they want to be, so use that.

Men are basically goldfish but with slightly longer memories. If you went on holiday and left a goldfish with enough food for two weeks it'd die cos they eat it all straight away. Now blokes are basically the same but with girls not food. If there's a girl near a guy who's had a drink and she looks like she'll have sex with him he'll go for it. He won't remember he's got a girlfriend if she's further away than the girl he can see. I reckon if you could get enough different women to keep entering a bloke's eye-line who were willing he'd fuck himself to death just through forgetting what he'd just done. Like the goldfish but I guess kind of the opposite because he'd be . . . Well the opposite of too full.

There was this guy I liked at work, not like like liked him but he was good-looking, funny. It was our Christmas do, we'd hit this target, smashed this target so they'd laid on this club and food and champagne and everyone's giving it the big un and I felt . . . I just feel really lonely and this chap Tom, the guy I liked, kind of liked he'd moved away from the group he was with, he went to the bar to buy drinks. Well I say buy drinks, they were free, well on the firm whatever but he was getting the drinks and I . . . I moved towards him, went to the bar just like I was just going to the bar as though I was going to get a drink and made sure I got there at the same time as him and I'm stood beside him and he sees me. 'Rachel ma belle sont des mots that go together well,' he sings, that's what he always does when he sees me and I'm like, 'It's Mi-Chelle' and he's

'No you're Rachel.' I know I said he was funny but that's probably not the best example.

I move in as he speaks, it's loud, the music's loud in the club so moving in makes sense so we can hear each other. As he speaks, he speaks with his hands. I don't mean signing, he's not deaf, but like he's expressive he moves his hands as he's telling you something. He'd put a beer down to tell a funny story cos I guess he knows that he's gonna have to move his hands a certain way to tell a punchline even though it's just words. I move in towards him as he's moving his hands and talking and so his hands, he hasn't done this on purpose but the way I've moved forwards mean his hands are just resting in to my chest. He realises this and then realises I don't mind. I knew he had a girlfriend.

Suddenly I'm walking away and he's following not far behind, there's this wide kind of corridor bit that leads through to the loos and there's a payphone. We're in that bit together just the two of us and we're snogging and laughing a bit, not badly, not like laughing at each other or anyone but just snogging and messing around, I think he put his hand in my dress a bit. Wouldn't have gone too far then . . . Then this lady comes out the toilets and says 'Tom?' then just stares at us and he goes completely still. And she's staring, not the way blokes stare at something they want or you might glance at a Belgian bun, she looks really sad, like something's died in her and she walks away and Tom looks at me. He looks at me and he glares really beyond glares looks at me like I'm scum, utter utter . . . And he runs off after her. I didn't know she was there, I didn't know she worked at the same firm. But I feel way lonelier now than I had done before.

Scene Nine

Rachel I remember the first time I met her. By her you know who I mean, I can't call her case one one-seventeen that's just fucking weird, I'll call her . . . Let's call her Marcia. It was one of those addresses that just isn't there. I mean you look at it on Google maps and it tells you the way then there just isn't a street where the map says it is. I was late, I ended up late because to get to this place you had to literally walk a quarter of a mile around two different side roads to get to this place. Most of the places around that side were churches, well they were called churches weren't really what you'd think of as a church, no steeples, just a load of incense inside an old cricket bat factory, but people lived there, well they were there all the time and they called it a church.

So I've got around the back, I phoned them and they've told me how to get there, 'You have to go around the back.' they say, so I do. I get around there and there's literally just a fire in the street that no one seemed to have an eye on at all but didn't look like it would get out of hand. Definitely man-made, not like something had caught alight. Nothing major but still just in the middle of the street there's a fire and no one bats an eye.

So I had about five minutes there in the end, it's all I could do. It had taken me that long to get there and I knew I'd be as late again finding my way back out to make it on to the next place so I pop in, the mum was nice, says hello and that, friendly. Baby was asleep in the cot, saw her face she looked all right, healthy and that. I could smell weed, it could have been from outside, nothing lit in the room I was in and no smoke in the air but somebody had obviously had a joint not too long ago but if we pull up everyone where that's the case, well . . . Well we can't, we just couldn't do that. Everything was fine though and I knew next time I'd get a better chance to have a longer chat and what have ya but that's the way it was that day.

Scene Ten

Rachel   Bonus. IPI got a new director and his job was to 'Make sure we are milking each cow for all it has in the udder and then some.' Most people hated him, he was all right, to me. Pretty fast he put me in charge of the team which meant I had to retrain Sarah who'd got me the job as she just wasn't making enough sales, people hated me for this. But I was put on a proper wage and earning another thousand pounds a week in bonus on top. I asked how long they thought this could last and was asked, 'How long can you keep pumping those udders?'

I could do nice things. I could go to restaurants I wanted to eat at. I could go on proper holidays and not have to fly at four o'clock in the morning on a plane that even girls half my size couldn't fit their legs into. I could buy all the things that I wanted, which was mainly wine and my own flat.

But someone phoned back, nobody had ever called back. I mean we call out on a London number so people know to answer the phone, that it's not a robot thing. But nobody had ever asked for me by name. An older lady, not old but . . . sixties? I pulled her details up and as I looked at the info on the screen I did remember the call. We were offered double commission on package covering loss not theft. She'd lost her phone. Again. Something she'd told me before she does fairly often so had been an easy sale for me. Thing was the insurance we'd sold her paid out once you produced a crime reference number and the police wouldn't give her a crime reference number on the basis that no crime had taken place.

I could see what they were doing, getting us to push that. You offer a deal knowing that people won't be able to claim in the only way you've made them entitled to. And I'd helped them do it. More than helped, pushed.

Angela her name was, her calling back made me realise, not only was I not helping people, I was actually stopping them getting what they were entitled to and in the process causing pointless work for police who could actually be helping people otherwise. Stayed with me that.

Scene Eleven

Rachel   Dry. January. Day two of. January second. It was a small step. I wanted to make it though. A tiny step on what would hopefully be a journey towards becoming a good person, well a better person. There's a lady I always see by the cashpoint outside the Tesco and on the evenings she's there asking for change. Quietly, never hassles anyone she just sits there and I never give her anything. 'Sorry,' I say and she'll smile and say 'Thank you' usually, just pleased someone's acknowledged her but I never give her anything. I've got the money, I make a lot of money, I make more money than I need but I just don't give any away. I spend it, shoes, drinks, food, stuff.

Today I walk past the lady and she's saying 'Any spare change?' and I give her two pounds, just hand her the coins and she says 'Thank you' and I smile, but I don't feel any better. About myself. I just wanna feel a bit better about myself, like anything I do makes a difference even the smallest difference to someone for the better. When I got in I poured a glass of wine. I always pour a glass of wine when I come in. I'd drunk from it before I'd even remembered I was supposed to be doing the whole dry January . . . Bollocks, oh well, I can do something though. It was partly I couldn't face going back to IPI, the bitchy fucking whispers since the Christmas do. I Googled, I searched online 'care', 'making a difference', and there were some jobs that had that. Said that. Said that they offered that. Didn't offer much money, but I've got money, but I wanted that, what they were offering. I started kind of filling out the online form.

Scene Twelve

Rachel   'We're gonna get to meet the Queen,' a voice, a simpleton, sorry a not-very-good-at-the-job person says from other side of the room, I presume he's just either wrong, stupid, confused or a trio of the above. But he's right or it seems he's on the right track. We get an email out and it seems that we've received a Queen's Award for Industry and a royal representative is coming around and we're all going to get a badge. My mum will go fucking nuts over this, she loves Liz Windsor. I call her Liz mainly because it gets my mum's back up. I call her and let her know, I'm meeting Liz Windsor, well the boss is, and I get one of her representatives coming around.

Mum's now got a photograph of me, me and the 'E' badge with a crown on it that you get given, she's got that picture in the downstairs loo, the one she makes guests use if they visit so she can always bring it up. It's odd cos when I told her about the job she didn't give a shit. I mean I told her what I was doing, which fair play, selling phone insurance is fucking boring. Even when I told her about the money I was earning she just said, 'Well that will do then until . . . ' Didn't say until what but I presume she would have finished the sentence with 'find a husband'. But when she found out the Palace were acknowledging the company and I was doing quite well there, she never wanted me to leave.

He had a sword the fella who came around, not sure if it was sharp, he had it in his . . . sheath? I spoke to him. 'You must be very proud' he says to me and I've never felt anything less. I can't change that message though. Help people and you're treated like an interfering busybody but money, money is something that should make you proud. Greed's not just good. Greed is everything.

Scene Thirteen

Rachel   I loved the people I was training with to get into social work. It's the first time I'd actually been in the same room as people who I actually thought wanted to be there and cared about the same thing. Even on my course at uni there seemed to be a fair amount of girls who'd just filled out the form because you have to fill out a UCAS form at school and so they'd ended up on a course where they'd have been better off getting a job in a clothes shop and focus on their real aims which were mainly getting pregnant. This was so different, actually learning stuff that is serious and can make a difference, it's pretty fucking scary but you . . . you start to believe in yourself, seeing people tell you stuff they expect you to be doing it was just . . . It felt right. You'd finish a day, knackered but good knackered like you'd actually done something with your brain and that was, that was worthwhile.

Closest to anything like this had been when IPI – oh I didn't say did I, Independent Phone Insurers was where I had worked we'd never call them IPI on the phone cos people hear PPI and just hang up on you but IPI had sent me on a course cos they needed someone to be the office first-aider and since I'd been there over three years I got sent along. I loved it in the end, initially I was just thinking about missing bonus but I realised this was something might save someone's life. A girl on that course was like, 'Look I don't give a fuck I just need to pass the certificate so our office is legally compliant or whatever,' made no sense to me that. If you can learn something that might save a life, why wouldn't you wanna be as best informed you could be?

That is why I fucking loved the attitude of everyone I was training here with. Sally sat next to me, lovely girl. I say girl older than me but not . . . Not like old. Everyone working hard but just . . . together not against each other.

Scene Fourteen

Rachel   January first, a day of new beginnings innit. A fresh start, wipe the slate clean, throw the old calendar away, the one full of family birthdays that you wrote in to remind yourself and still forgot to send a card in time for.

This is years back, the one after the Christmas party where I snogged that knobhead. I was drinking . . . I know this, I know this because of the calendar actually the one I threw away that day. It had various Christmas dos and other things logged in there like my friend Lucy's birthday, her birthday's day before Christmas Eve so no one's ever free for it so I always make sure I get pissed with her the two of us. So from the events marked on the calendar and other things I just remember I'd been drinking hard for ten days straight.

So that January first I've woken up and I'm not just what you'd say is hungover, I'm . . . I'm in a bad way. I wake up and initially it just feels like, well, like things felt every morning. Head hurts, feel sick but neither of them's the worst bit, it's the constant feeling of regret or guilt like there is something you've done what you shouldn't have done but you can't remember what it is which only makes it much worse in your mind.

That morning I was sick. I'd not been sick for about ten years, not from alcohol. Sounds weird but when I'd been sick in my teens from booze it had panicked me, scared me thinking I'd choke on it in my sleep or something. So my brain it had a kind of, agreement. Like I had an agreement with my head, don't be sick, keep it in, keep it down, you can feel as bad as you like but keep it down. I'm looking at my sick and I'm thinking what the fuck have I drunk? So I try to remind myself and this makes me feel worse. You can try and tell yourself sometimes that you've not drunk that much, see if you can trick your brain into feeling better but today, no. Today there's no lying because today I can remember because I went out that New Year's Eve with a plan. Two of my old housemates from first year have got a place together still and having house party at theirs. Suzie, one of them, text'd me about it and I've not organised anything else to do and it's December thirtieth so I says yeah I'll meet up with you tomorrow, but because we've not seen each other for a while I'll meet you beforehand before it gets into . . . carnage.

So we meet up earlier in the day and they've not done the shopping yet and so we go supermarket, the big one with the . . . it's on like a hill like one of them American-style places with car park and that and we start buying stuff, I weigh in paying, no problem, I'll drink my fair share I says, laughing a bit too hard. And we buy everything. Well, boozewise we buy everything, every booze then six packets of crisps, big packs, and them spicy nuts. And I went into this thing in my head, I'm not tight, not tight at all but I just went into this thing that because I'd paid a share of everything I should have one of everything. So I can't convince myself I've not had a lot to drink cos I know. I know I've had, red wine, white wine, a beer, Guinness, I don't like Guinness at all but I just had it in my brain I had to have a different drink each time so . . . I followed that with a cider get the taste of Guinness away then a sherry, Chritmassy thing innit. Then a G and T, a light rum and Coke, a dark rum and lemonade then someone's brought some . . . I don't know what it is but their family's from Lebanon and they've given 'em some lemon sort of fire stuff for Christmas and I've had a shot of that, it's tough on your throat so I've had a brandy to follow then it's midnight and we're popping the champagne and cava whatever so I've had a glass then they're cocktailing that so I've had a Kir Royale, then I'm just drinking vodka from a bottle and I'm crying in the garden for a bit, can't remember the bit in between cocktails and that. Then some lad Suzie knows is trying to kiss me and I've stopped crying and I've probably snogged him for a bit, but I don't really know him or fancy him even. I'm inside and drinking whisky now, then I must have just decided to leave because I'm at home and there's crisps everywhere, I must have passed out.

So now it's January first and I'm being sick and I've got this horrible guilt feeling running through me but I have to leave the house and go for a walk cos I remember, stupid plan but I remember Suzie and a couple of pals have said they're gonna do this walk over Regent's Park and I'm so shakey, feeling so like I've done something bad that I've got it in my brain that I can't let 'em down, like if I didn't go there I'd be a horrible person. So I go and I meet them, she's got these two friends bit older, I think a bit older . . . Whatever, they're definitely you know, sorted, they've got kids. And they're really nice and they do things for each other and for other people, like that Christmas they'd got a load of stuff from neighbours for a food bank and gathered warm clothes and sheets for anyone having to sleep rough. As well as having a fucking baby they still think about other people and they ask me what I do and all I wanna say is 'I con people on the phone for work and socially get off with other girls' boyfriends' but what comes out is 'I currently help people sort out their what's its if their phone gets damaged . . . But I'm looking to move into social care.'

And these people they look impressed by this, these kind people look at me, this hungover wreck and see me as one of them. As better even, someone who is looking to go full time into helping people. And Suzie looks at me like . . . like she doesn't wanna call me a liar but thinks I'm maybe mistaken in what I've said and she's like, 'That's a long way from what we studied.' Actually I didn't mention did I. My degree's in fashion.

Scene Fifteen

Rachel   The cat-in-the-bin lady I blame her, well I don't blame her but she's basically the person who made trolling OK. Made it mainstream. Bullying, it is essentially bullying, but on a massive massive level and people are OK with it. It's like if in a film they wanna do something really bad to someone you make them a Nazi then people watching are basically OK with it. Whatever's done to them they're not seen as human any more, they become something other.

That's what the cat lady did, before her I can't remember anyone, anyone normal who it suddenly became OK to wish really really horrible stuff on. Now don't get me wrong, I'm not for trapping cats in bins. If there was a survey tomorrow and I'm asked do cats belong in A) the bin or B) anywhere other than that I'd be with B every time. Although I don't mean I want cats in a cement mixer or anything like that either. By B I mean anything within reason, anywhere reasonable for a cat to be.

The lady should not have put the cat in that bin let's be clear on that but she's just a woman who did a really stupid horrible thing. It was the wrong thing to do and she shouldn't have done it but for a country to turn . . . For every Facebook, Twitter everything online to be like a proper witch hunt, like a proper 'let's burn her at the stake' deal . . . Well that can't be right either. Suddenly people are like, 'Let's put her in a bin,' 'Binning is too good for her,' hunting her down trying to find out where she lives or whatever and people. I mean people I'm actually friends with, are liking this. They're clicking like or making their own comments about what needs to be done to this sad disturbed lady. I mean she needed help, you don't do stuff like that if you've not got problems, things that need dealing with.

Suddenly you've got someone who's other, not a person, not someone who is there in front of you and you would try to reason with or help. Suddenly it's OK to unleash all the darkness all the horrible things people have deep in the back of their mind that should stay there . . . Well suddenly you can write that stuff, say that stuff. She was the pioneer of that and I reaped the benefits.

Scene Sixteen

Rachel   This woman is nice, Marcia. I mean really nice, she is friendly and she is kind. We'd only really got to speak very briefly the first time I'd met her, few seconds on the phone then for a bit at the house but I was feeling rushed and she was a bit nervous but talking to her now, she is nice, she's so kind you just see it in her eyes but she has made some bad life choices. I mean we all wanna give people the benefit of the doubt but she is too trusting. She starts telling me about her life, she's twenty-eight and she's got six kids, set of twins in there but still . . . And she just trusts men. I'm not saying don't trust men, I'm not saying don't trust anyone, but as she's talking to me, as much as I like her I'm thinking, 'You fucking idiot why do you keep trusting people?' I'm still not . . . I still can't really go into this into too much about this but . . . Argh fuck it she just told me about the dads, the dads of her kids and each time, each time I'm thinking, wanna scream out at her. She just needed someone when she was a kid, a mum a dad a friend who would say to her, let her know. Things boys say. Things boys say to get ya into bed, things boys say once they've got ya into bed and things boys say which mean you'll never see them again, for dust.

And she'd heard them all, A to Z the whole fucking book and even some new ones, ones you'd wanna actually laugh at. Like you can't get pregnant from behind, I don't mean up the . . . I mean just doing it from behind, the fella's told her you can't get pregnant and she's believed him. Like the sperm would know. I wanted to laugh but . . . See after all the blokes who'd gone, all the lies, all the things the dads had said to her. Said they loved her, said they'd be there, that they'd support the baby, it was them against everything each of them had . . . And now she'd found the one, the one who wasn't going to go anywhere wasn't going to leave her, she'd not even had a kid with. She described this man and I knew I just knew he was the one she needed to be away from the most.

I drunk the tea, it was OK. I took the empty cup to the sink washed it up myself, she didn't want me to I insisted. The sink had an odd combination, smelt of lemons, like artificial lemons bleach, clean plates on the side but the food catcher thing you have to stop big bits running down the plughole was out on the side and had fungus actually growing in it.

Michael. Let's call him Michael or you might know him as 'the Stepfather' she mentioned him. I'm not going to tell you real names, even after everything. You know who I mean. I mean it's on Twitter and some cunt of a politician even used parliamentary fucking privilege to out her fucking name on camera, in the same breath as mine. Judge banned any pictures of them, not me though and people blame who they can see. Michael was different, she said, he was a good man, he was from the church, one of the churches, the incense ones, the old cricket bat factory. She'd not met him there but he lived there or . . . Well she was a little unclear on where he'd been *living* living but she knew he spent most of his time there until he'd . . . Decided the kids needed a role model in the home and he should be there for them and for her. And he was happy to make the sacrifice and join them so he could lead them on the right path.

Scene Seventeen

Rachel A lady wrote to me, wrote a letter. With pen. I know. I'd been working with her and I'm not gonna say what had happened to her but she really didn't think she'd ever have any hopes of forming a connection, romantically or even just a connection a decent friendship between her and another . . . Anyone. She wrote to me but the letter she sent, it wasn't to me it was a copy of a letter she'd sent, she'd written out a copy of a letter she sent to someone. See she'd found someone and she'd been able to open up to them. She'd not really been to school this girl so just writing at all was so . . . It touched me but reading her letter well. I remember it.

'Bertie' – that wasn't his name, don't know why I'm calling him that be honest but – 'Bertie, when I wake up life is normal and dull for a second then I remember you're in the world and I smile and I look beside me and if you're there beside me my heart leaps up to my eyes and my eyes smile as well and I want you to know that before I go to sleep at night I still feel that smile and love and hope in my heart because you love me. I will never be able to do enough to deserve the love you give to me but I will do all I can to keep that love between us each day from when I wake up and remember you to when I fall asleep and dream about you. Yours.'

She used to not be able to make eye-contact with me to say thank you if I poured her a cup of tea when we first met.

Scene Eighteen

Rachel I always felt trapped going home. I mean home home, Ashow, Mum and Dad's, firstly cos it's so fucking remote. There's a kind of church hall and that's pretty much it and a few houses. Nice place to bring kids up they say. I don't know. Away from crime and the city but you need to be near something.

Last time I stayed with them my auntie had died, Mum wanted me to be just . . . around, you know, just so she could have someone to tell they were doing stuff not quite the way she'd have done it. Dad goes into a kind of making mode when he's . . . It was his sister, but Mum seemed to take it worse, or spoke about it, crying what have you. Dad all he said was, 'They've made a right mess of that door when they've gone and collected her,' they must have kicked the door in when she wasn't answering the phone, and 'The back fence has come down.' The back fence was nothing to do with Auntie dying or anything else of much but Dad decided he had to get fixing.

He didn't say he was sad, it was his only sister or sibling. He didn't say he felt like there was anything he could have done, there wasn't anything he could have done, but he just got his toolbox and electric saws whatever he's got and he went over there and he fixed up that door frame and he fixed up the back fence and he called me over. He phoned me and said, 'Come over,' and I thought I was gonna talk to him about . . . I don't know something, either how he felt or even I don't know the will, something practical, but I came over when he called and all he said to me was, he showed me the door frame he'd fixed and he said, 'They won't knock that down again in a hurry.' And I leant on it and it was strong he was right. But they'd needed to be able to knock it down cos she was in there dead.

And I just had these three days up there before the funeral. Three days where Dad said nothing, nothing to me really except that, and Mum just following me round criticising any of the things she was making me do around the house. Laughing, laughing a fake laugh but making out, making out like it was the funniest thing in the world. 'Our Rachel's put the big knives in same drawer as the rolling pins, can you imagine?' I snapped a little at that, cos, what? and Mum's like 'Oh you're just like your father he hasn't a clue, not a clue where anything goes. I daren't die, he'd be putting things back in all the wrong places, he has a hard enough time finding things when I've put them in the right place can you imagine what he'd be like if I was gone?'

And that's the nicest time I've spent with them. Sounds horrible but it was OK, because in that horrible fucked-up way families show things to each other I knew they cared about me and wanted to show that they'd protect this family. Our family. Me.

Scene Nineteen

Rachel   Chased. Cameras snapping. Just lights, flashes and snap snap snap. Chasing, running. Me, alone you can see, men large men a group of them. I'm not a pop star, they're not trying to see up my skirt as I get in a car. They want blood. Pushing, saying things trying to get a reaction. 'Do you see yourself as directly responsible?' I was just walking fast really before but now, running. I'm really trying to get away but not sure why I'm bothering, just hope. Only hope keeps me going but where am I gonna go? More shouting, 'If you are deemed to be responsible in some part, should you be charged?' I trip a bit, keep running. Fucking heels not made for this. 'Are you sorry, Rachel?' I run full pelt now. As fast as I can go then I'm down, didn't feel like I tripped on something feels like something hit me but I look and my shoe's caught in a crack in the ground. I'm down on that same ground and they're around me and snapping. 'Get a tight shot on the blood' I hear a voice say and more snapping, I'm getting myself up, my legs cut. Over ten men right around me but not one with an arm free to lift me. I'm walking again but I can't remember which way I came from, not any idea now of where I am going but I see a road. Traffic oncoming. Them behind me . . . I step out.

'Taxi' I scream and he's seen me, he sees me and he stops. He stops and I'm in, I've got inside. 'Where to, love?' I don't know. I've no idea what to tell him. 'Just drive please.' I say, he sees the lights flashing, cameras snapping and he smiles at me, he smiles and drives. We get half a mile up the street and he looks in the mirror to check out who I am. 'Sung anything my daughter would know?' 'Eh?' I says. 'Singer are you?' He doesn't know me, doesn't recognise me. 'I had that one off the *X Factor* in the back the other week, all them same bastards chasing her out that one on Dean Street, Grouchies . . . The Gr . . . the Grinch Club . . . ? You know the one?' 'I'm not a singer, I'm afraid, so . . . ' We drive along for a bit. 'Absolute bastards them fellas, utter scum. I know they'll say they've got a job to do but . . . If no one was prepared to do it, if no one was prepared to say yeah I'll chase someone down the street in a gang with our cameras, going through dustbins, we wouldn't miss it would we?' I smile. 'Take me for example, now if all the cabbies, if we stop doing this well people wouldn't be able to get anywhere would they, like people would start charging for lifts and make a business out of it, cabs would just exist in a new way like . . . ' 'Uber?' I say, he glares. 'But if nobody waited at airports to see the moment someone was told their wife had died so they could get the first picture of them as they get off the plane well . . . Well, we wouldn't miss that would we?' I nod. 'You got anywhere I should drop you. love?' I don't know why I said this but . . . 'Waterloo Bridge' comes out my mouth, he shrugs and makes a U-turn without checking traffic on either side. 'What's it you do then? You one of these reality stars?' I receive the question and, 'Yeah. I guess I am in a way,' I've replied. Then I'm on the bridge. The water and you can look out and there's St Paul's and the Wheel and all the beautiful things I got excited by when I first moved here and just for that moment, everything is OK.

Scene Twenty

Rachel   I'd stopped drinking. Not like an alcoholic, not like I had to stop or anything, I just did. Partly the hours I was keeping meant by the time I got home I was almost going straight to bed. I've never drunk when I'm working anyway and doing stuff that really matters that you really care about well . . . There was no way I'd have like a glass of wine with lunch, not that I had lunch anyway if I was going to have several cases on the afternoon. In sales it wasn't much different to uni really except you were drinking somewhere much more expensive and often nicer but once I'd left both those things behind I also . . . I just didn't want to drink initially.

I saw this advert on the Tube and it said 'Thinking of helping others in the coming year? Become a sperm donor.' I saw that and didn't just feel the obvious, well I can't help in that anyway but actually for the first time felt I was making a difference in a better way. I wasn't having to make up an excuse in my mind why I should't be giving to this charity or that one I was actually helping people. So I wasn't drinking.

Scene Twenty-One

Rachel   Enter the room. I sit here. I'm sat here. I'm ready for this. Fuck you. Fuck you for not protecting me, fuck you for not giving me facility to protect the people I was trying to and fuck you for doing this whole fucking thing so you can cover your own arses.

'Thank you for coming in,' he says. 'I understand you've been having quite a time of it and we're sorry about that, what we're hoping today is we can work out what went . . . What we can help with and how we move forward from here and hopefully get you back to work as soon as . . . Yes.'

And then he just talks and he keeps talking, sometimes they sound like questions but there's no way for me to answer them they're like, 'So you were given the training and had it explained to you clearly the procedure to . . . ?' And I'm saying yes and he's ticking boxes and moving on but I'm just thinking, thinking about what happened.

Then they're asking me to wait outside, thanking me for my time and saying they need to confirm a few issues and if I wouldn't mind waiting out . . . And I'm back outside again and all the things I'd meant to say, to explain to . . . Fuck you to them I haven't done and I'm just back waiting in the chair and the security fella nods at me then gets on with whatever it is they pretend to look at on their screens.

Scene Twenty-Two

Rachel   She said she'd got rid of Michael, that he wasn't living with them any more. I couldn't blame her, for that and . . . I still don't blame *her*. There was something different in Marcia at this point, she'd always seemed a bit tired, not abnormally so, can't't imagine how I'd get on with all those kids, me bringing them up on my own, well alone most of the time. But her face that day, if there was an image the world was allowed, if it wasn't only pictures of me people associate with all this, well, her face that that day would be it. She didn't seem upset. I went through and the kids were all playing a computer game in the other room, well two of them were, three of them were watching. The baby wasn't there 'She's with her auntie.' She'd never mentioned an auntie before. 'Your sister?' I ask. 'Yes, she's my good sister,' and the other kids are fine like they play fight, the boys they bash around with each other like . . . like you'd expect kids to do so they're not, couldn't say I never saw a bruise on one of them can't say none of them ever had a cold or could have been eating better, bit more healthily but what can you . . . ? Do you take a kid off his mother for that? Have brothers and sisters separated growing up apart not getting to see each other? They were always happy, they loved each other. She just trusted men, trusted all the wrong men and I never . . . The baby. That little girl, she'd always be dressed nicely and I wasn't gonna go taking off her outfits, the time it'd take and she was always smiling and laughing and fine and then . . . Then she just said Michael was gone and the baby was with her sister, then the next time the auntie wasn't her sister she said it was a friend or that she'd always said that, that she was on holiday with a friend. A nice lady, a lady from the church. But she wasn't on holiday, she'd never left that flat. Well, at that point most of her was still in the flat. I wouldn't have started if I knew this was the end.

Finish.

Bloomsbury Methuen Drama Modern Plays

include work by

Bola Agbaje
Edward Albee
Davey Anderson
Jean Anouilh
John Arden
Peter Barnes
Sebastian Barry
Alistair Beaton
Brendan Behan
Edward Bond
William Boyd
Bertolt Brecht
Howard Brenton
Amelia Bullmore
Anthony Burgess
Leo Butler
Jim Cartwright
Lolita Chakrabarti
Caryl Churchill
Lucinda Coxon
Curious Directive
Nick Darke
Shelagh Delaney
Ishy Din
Claire Dowie
David Edgar
David Eldridge
Dario Fo
Michael Frayn
John Godber
Paul Godfrey
James Graham
David Greig
John Guare
Mark Haddon
Peter Handke
David Harrower
Jonathan Harvey
Iain Heggie

Robert Holman
Caroline Horton
Terry Johnson
Sarah Kane
Barrie Keeffe
Doug Lucie
Anders Lustgarten
David Mamet
Patrick Marber
Martin McDonagh
Arthur Miller
D. C. Moore
Tom Murphy
Phyllis Nagy
Anthony Neilson
Peter Nichols
Joe Orton
Joe Penhall
Luigi Pirandello
Stephen Poliakoff
Lucy Prebble
Peter Quilter
Mark Ravenhill
Philip Ridley
Willy Russell
Jean-Paul Sartre
Sam Shepard
Martin Sherman
Wole Soyinka
Simon Stephens
Peter Straughan
Kate Tempest
Theatre Workshop
Judy Upton
Timberlake Wertenbaker
Roy Williams
Snoo Wilson
Frances Ya-Chu Cowhig
Benjamin Zephaniah

Bloomsbury Methuen Drama Contemporary Dramatists

include

Bloomsbury Methuen Drama Student Editions

Jean Anouilh *Antigone* • John Arden *Serjeant Musgrave's Dance* • Alan Ayckbourn *Confusions* • Aphra Behn *The Rover* • Edward Bond *Lear* • *Saved* • Bertolt Brecht *The Caucasian Chalk Circle* • *Fear and Misery in the Third Reich* • *The Good Person of Szechwan* • *Life of Galileo* • *Mother Courage and Her Children* • *The Resistible Rise of Arturo Ui* • *The Threepenny Opera* • Anton Chekhov *The Cherry Orchard* • *The Seagull* • *Three Sisters* • *Uncle Vanya* • Caryl Churchill *Serious Money* • *Top Girls* • Shelagh Delaney *A Taste of Honey* • Euripides *Elektra* • *Medea* • Dario Fo *Accidental Death of an Anarchist* • Michael Frayn *Copenhagen* • John Galsworthy *Strife* • Nikolai Gogol *The Government Inspector* • Carlo Goldoni *A Servant to Two Masters* • Lorraine Hansberry *A Raisin in the Sun* • Robert Holman *Across Oka* • Henrik Ibsen *A Doll's House* • *Ghosts* • *Hedda Gabler* • Sarah Kane *4.48 Psychosis* • *Blasted* • Charlotte Keatley *My Mother Said I Never Should* • Bernard Kops *Dreams of Anne Frank* • Federico García Lorca *Blood Wedding* • *Doña Rosita the Spinster* (bilingual edition) • *The House of Bernarda Alba* (bilingual edition) • *Yerma* (bilingual edition) • David Mamet *Glengarry Glen Ross* • *Oleanna* • Patrick Marber *Closer* • John Marston *The Malcontent* • Martin McDonagh *The Lieutenant of Inishmore* • *The Lonesome West* • *The Beauty Queen of Leenane* • Arthur Miller *All My Sons* • *The Crucible* • *A View from the Bridge* • *Death of a Salesman* • *The Price* • *After the Fall* • *The Last Yankee* • *A Memory of Two Mondays* • *Broken Glass* • Joe Orton *Loot* • Joe Penhall *Blue/Orange* • Luigi Pirandello *Six Characters in Search of an Author* • Lucy Prebble *Enron* • Mark Ravenhill *Shopping and F***ing* • Willy Russell *Blood Brothers* • *Educating Rita* • Sophocles *Antigone* • *Oedipus the King* • Wole Soyinka *Death and the King's Horseman* • Shelagh Stephenson *The Memory of Water* • August Strindberg *Miss Julie* • J. M. Synge *The Playboy of the Western World* • Theatre Workshop *Oh What a Lovely War* • Frank Wedekind *Spring Awakening* • Timberlake Wertenbaker *Our Country's Good* • Arnold Wesker *The Merchant* • Oscar Wilde *The Importance of Being Earnest* • Tennessee Williams *A Streetcar Named Desire* • *The Glass Menagerie* • *Cat on a Hot Tin Roof* • *Sweet Bird of Youth*